Trumpet Chants

This book contains 30 original "chants" composed for solo trumpet. The pieces are lyrical in nature and may be used in a variety of settings. They work well as a prelude or call to worship or even as recital selections, concert pieces or as encores to performances. These chants require sensitivity in interpretation and phrasing, a full, rich tone and control over breathing and volume. They also serve as good daily practice pieces. I hope you enjoy these solos as much as I have in writing and performing them.

William Bay

© 2016 by William Bay. All Rights Reserved.
Sales Agent: Mel Bay Publications, Inc.
www.melbay.com

Chant 1

Chant 2

Chant 3

Slowly, Freely ♩= 68

William Bay

Chant 4

William Bay

Chant 5

Chant 6

Chant 7

Chant 8

Chant 9

Chant 10

Chant 11

Chant 12

Chant 13

Chant 14

Chant 15

William Bay

Chant 16

Chant 17

Chant 18

Chant 19

Chant 20

Chant 21

Chant 22

Chant 23

Chant 24

Chant 25

William Bay

Chant 26

Chant 27

Chant 28

Chant 29

Chant 30